Learn to Crochet, NOW!

Learn how to crochet and make your first project at the same time with the sampler spa cloth! The clear, step by step instructions with right and left hand illustrations will have you crocheting in no time at all. Plus, we have made videos of all the basic stitches so you can watch over the shoulder of our crochet expert!

Contents

LEISURE ARTS, INC
Maumelle, Arkansas

2

26

28

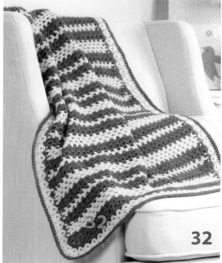

32

32

Learn to crochet your first project!

SPA CLOTH

By following the instructions, you will learn the basic stitches and have your first finished project.

First, gather the supplies you will need!

Take a look at the Shopping List. This appears at the beginning of all our projects. You only need 3 things.

SHOPPING LIST

Yarn (Medium Weight Cotton)

[3.5 ounces, 207 yards

(100 grams, 188 meters) per skein]:

☐ 1 skein

Crochet Hook

☐ Size H (5 mm)

Additional Supplies

☐ Yarn needle for hiding yarn ends

1. Yarn — a medium or worsted weight cotton yarn is what we used. This kind of yarn will give the best result for your spa cloth. Choose a light, bright color so it will be easier to see your stitches while you are learning.

2. Crochet Hook — hooks come in different sizes and are made from metal, plastic, or bamboo. For this project, use a size H (5 mm).

3. Yarn Needle— a yarn needle will have a large eye and a blunt tip and is used to weave the yarn ends into the cloth.

Now, you're ready to start!

Watch videos of the stitches and techniques taught on pages 4-19 at www.leisurearts.com/5947

Here's how to hold your Hook.

Hold your hook either like a table knife *(Fig. 1a)* or like a pencil *(Fig. 1b)*. Find the way that is most comfortable for you.

Fig. 1a Right-handed

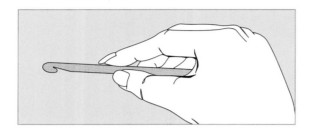

Fig. 1a Left-handed

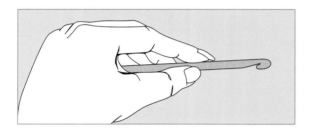

Fig. 1b Right-handed

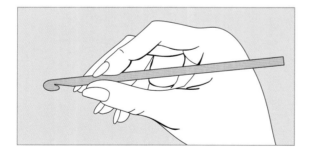

Fig. 1b Left-handed

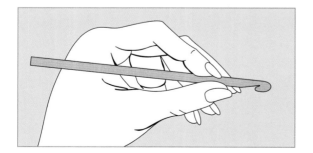

Make a Slip Knot.

Before learning how to hold the yarn, let's make a slip knot to place on your hook. Pull a length of yarn from the skein. Make a circle on top of the yarn that comes from the skein about 6" (15 cm) from the end *(Fig. 2a)*. The yarn that comes from the skein is called the working yarn and the other end is the tail.

Fig. 2a Right-handed

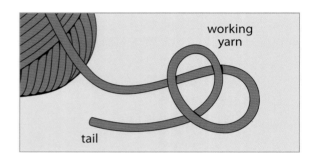

Fig. 2a Left-handed

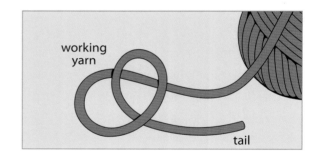

Slip your hook under the strand in the middle of the circle *(Fig. 2b)* and pull on both strands to tighten the knot on your hook *(Fig. 2c)*. The slip knot should slide easily up and down your hook, so adjust it if it is too tight.

Fig. 2b   Right-handed

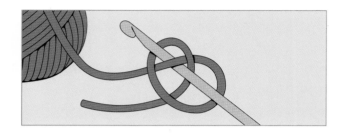

Fig. 2b   Left-handed

Fig. 2c   Right-handed

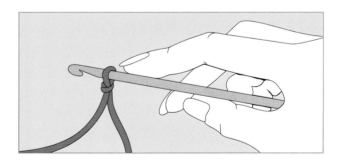

Fig. 2c   Left-handed

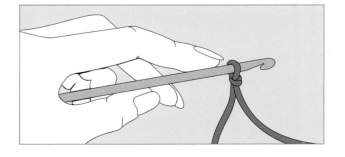

Here's how to hold your Yarn.

Hold the hook in your hand. Lay the working yarn over the index finger of your other hand. Hold the slip knot with the thumb and middle finger of that hand and fold your other fingers over the yarn in your palm *(Fig. 3)*. Just allow the yarn to move smoothly through your fingers without letting it get stretched.

Fig. 3   Right-handed

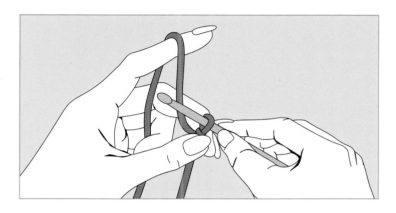

Fig. 3   Left-handed

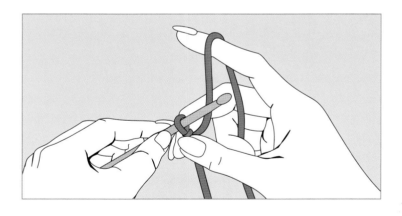

As you crochet, you will work with the section of the yarn between your index finger and the hook. If you find a different way of holding the yarn that is more comfortable for you, feel free to do it your way.

First, make a Yarn Over with your Hook (abbreviated YO).

Bring the working yarn over your hook from the **back** to the **front** *(Fig. 4)*. Catch the yarn with your hook and turn it slightly toward you so the yarn doesn't slip off. The yarn over is used in **every** crochet stitch.

Fig. 4   Right-handed

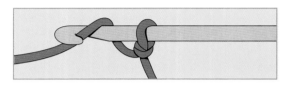

Fig. 4   Left-handed

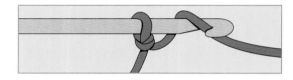

Next, make a Chain (abbreviated ch).

A chain is the beginning of every crochet project. Begin with a yarn over *(Fig. 4)*. To complete the first chain, draw the hook with its loop of yarn through the slip knot, following the direction of the arrow in **Fig. 5a**.

Fig. 5a   Right-handed

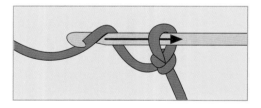

Fig. 5a   Left-handed

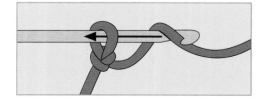

You have made the first chain and there will be one loop on your hook *(Fig. 5b)*.

Fig. 5b   Right-handed

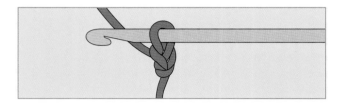

Fig. 5b   Left-handed

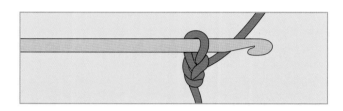

For each additional chain, bring the yarn over your hook from the **back** to the **front**, then draw the hook through the loop on the hook. Practice making the chains even and not too tight. The chains need to be large enough to put your hook back through them to create the stitches.

How to count your Chains.

When counting your chains, start at the first chain after the hook and count back to the slip knot *(Fig. 6)*.

Fig. 6   Right-handed

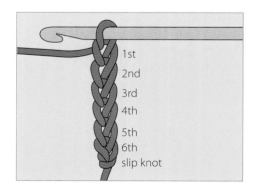

Fig. 6   Left-handed

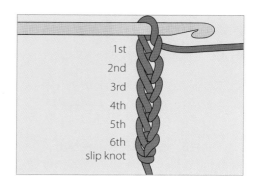

1st
2nd
3rd
4th
5th
6th
slip knot

Here's how to work into the loops of your Chain.

Insert the hook under the top two strands of each chain as indicated by the arrows *(Fig. 8)*.

Fig. 8   Right-handed

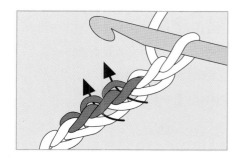

Chain 23 to begin your Spa Cloth.

Look at your Chain.

Once your chain is complete, you will work crochet stitches into the individual chains. Compare your chain to the one in Fig. 7. The top of your chain looks like a series of V's.

Fig. 8   Left-handed

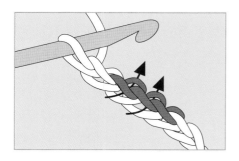

Fig. 7   Right-handed

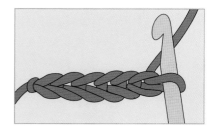

Fig. 7   Left-handed

Remember, you can watch each technique online!
www.leisurearts.com/5947

As you go along, you will notice that all of the stitches are similar—you will use yarn overs to create loops on your hook and then draw the yarn through those loops to complete the stitches. The more loops you have, the taller the stitch will be.

The Spa Cloth is worked in rows and you will learn the following stitches:
1. Single Crochet
2. Half Double Crochet
3. Double Crochet
4. Treble Crochet

Start with single crochets, *(abbreviated sc)*.

ROW 1

Insert your hook into the second chain from your hook *(Fig. 8, page 7)*.

Bring the yarn over your hook *(Fig. 4, page 6)*. Draw your hook through the chain, following the direction of the arrow *(Fig. 9a)*, pulling up a loop.

Fig. 9a   Right-handed

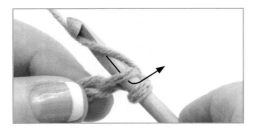

Fig. 9a   Left-handed

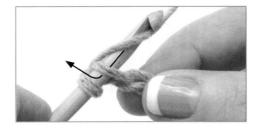

You will have 2 loops on your hook *(Fig. 9b)*.

Fig. 9b   Right-handed

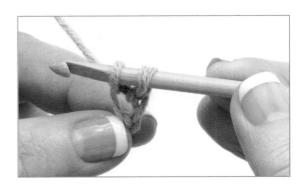

Fig. 9b   Left-handed

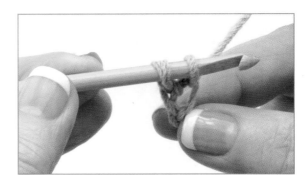

Bring the yarn over your hook and draw the hook through both loops on your hook, completing your first single crochet *(Fig. 9c)*.

Fig. 9c   Right-handed

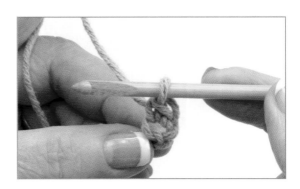

Fig. 9c   Left-handed

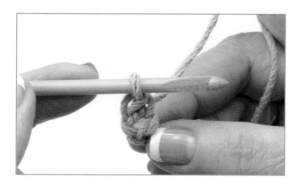

Following the steps in **Figs. 9a-c**, work a single crochet in each chain across your beginning chain. At the end of Row 1, you will have 22 single crochets.

Count your stitches by looking at their top loops—they will look like your chain. Each stitch will have a V-shape at the top.

Right-handed

1st

Left-handed

1st

ROW 2

Chain 1; then turn your work around *(Fig. 9d)*.

Fig. 9d   Right-handed

Fig. 9d   Left-handed

Following the steps in **Figs. 9a-c**, work a single crochet in the first single crochet and in each single crochet across; at the end of Row 2, you will have 22 single crochets.

ROW 3

Repeat Row 2; at the end of the Row 3, you will have 22 single crochets.

Learn a little taller stitch, the half double crochet *(abbreviated hdc)*!

ROW 4

To start your first row of half double crochets, chain 2. These 2 chains will count as the first half double crochet. Turn your work around *(Fig. 10a)*.

Fig. 10a   Right-handed

Fig. 10a   Left-handed

Bring the yarn over your hook. Skip the first single crochet on the previous row and insert your hook in the next single crochet *(Fig. 10b)*.

Fig. 10b   Right-handed

Fig. 10b   Left-handed

Bring the yarn over your hook and draw the hook through the stitch, pulling up a loop. You will have 3 loops on your hook *(Fig. 10c)*.

Fig. 10c   Right-handed

Fig. 10c Left-handed

Bring the yarn over your hook and draw through all 3 loops on your hook, completing the half double crochet *(Fig. 10d)*.

Fig. 10d Right-handed

Fig. 10d Left-handed

Following the steps in **Figs. 10b-d**, work a half double crochet in the next single crochet and in each single crochet across; at the end of Row 4, you will have 22 half double crochets including the beginning chain 2.

ROW 5

Chain 2 (**counts as the first half double crochet**); turn your work around. Skip the first half double crochet on the previous row and work a half double crochet in the next half double crochet and in each half double crochet across to the last half double crochet (the turning chain 2 of the previous row). Work your last half double crochet in the top of the chain 2 *(Fig. 10e)*. You will have 22 half double crochets.

Fig. 10e Right-handed

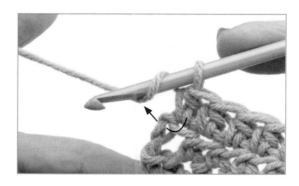

Fig. 10e Left-handed

ROWS 6 AND 7

Repeat Row 5 twice; at the end of each row, you will have 22 half double crochets.

ROW 8

Chain 1; turn your work around. Work a single crochet *(Figs. 9a-c, pages 8 and 9)* in the first half double crochet and in each half double crochet across; at the end of the row, you will have 22 single crochets.

Learn an even taller stitch, the double crochet *(abbreviated dc)*!

ROW 9

To start your first row of double crochets, chain 3. These 3 chains will count as the first double crochet. Turn your work around *(Fig. 11a)*.

Fig. 11a   Right-handed

Fig. 11a   Left-hand

Bring the yarn over your hook. Skip the first single crochet on the previous row and insert your hook in the next single crochet *(Fig. 11b)*.

Fig. 11b   Right-handed

Fig. 11b Left-handed

Bring the yarn over your hook and draw the hook through the stitch, pulling up a loop. You will have 3 loops on your hook *(Fig. 11c)*.

Fig. 11c   Right-handed

Fig. 11c Left-handed

Bring the yarn over your hook and draw through the first 2 loops on the hook. You will have 2 loops remaining on your hook *(Fig. 11d)*.

Fig. 11d Right-handed

Fig. 11d Left-handed

Bring the yarn over your hook and draw through the last 2 loops on your hook, completing the double crochet *(Fig. 11e)*.

Fig. 11e Right-handed

Fig. 11e Left-handed

Following the steps in **Figs. 11b-e**, work a double crochet in the next single crochet and in each single crochet across. At the end of Row 9, you will have 22 double crochets including the beginning chain 3.

Remember, you can watch each technique online!
www.leisurearts.com/5947

ROW 10

Chain 3 (**counts as the first double crochet**); turn your work around. Skip the first double crochet on the previous row and work a double crochet in the next double crochet and in each double crochet across to the last double crochet (the turning chain 3 of the previous row). Work your last double crochet in the top of the chain 3 *(Fig. 11f)*. You will have 22 double crochets.

Fig. 11f   Right-handed

Fig. 11f   Left-handed

ROWS 11 AND 12

Repeat Row 10 twice; at the end of each row, you will have 22 double crochets.

ROW 13

Chain 1; turn your work around. Work a single crochet *(Figs. 9a-c, pages 8 and 9)* in the first double crochet and in each double crochet across; at the end of Row 13, you will have 22 single crochets.

Here's a very tall stitch to learn, the treble crochet *(abbreviated tr)*!

ROW 14

To start your first row of treble crochets, chain 4. These 4 chains will count as the first treble crochet. Turn your work around *(Fig. 12a)*.

Fig. 12a   Right-handed

Fig. 12a   Left-handed

Bring the yarn over your hook twice. Skip the first single crochet on the previous row and insert your hook in the next single crochet *(Fig. 12b)*.

Fig. 12b   Right-handed

Fig. 12b   Left-handed

Bring the yarn over your hook and draw the hook through the stitch, pulling up a loop. You will have 4 loops on your hook *(Fig. 12c)*.

Fig. 12c   Right-handed

Fig. 12c   Left-handed

Bring the yarn over your hook and draw through the first 2 loops on the hook. You will have 3 loops remaining on your hook *(Fig. 12d)*.

Fig. 12d   Right-handed

Fig. 12d   Left-handed

Bring the yarn over your hook and draw through the next 2 loops on your hook. You will have 2 loops remaining on your hook (*Fig. 12e*).

Fig. 12e   Right-handed

Fig. 12e   Left-handed

Bring the yarn over your hook and draw through the remaining 2 loops on your hook, completing the treble crochet (*Fig. 12f*).

Fig. 12f   Right-handed

Fig. 12f   Left-handed

Following the steps in **Figs. 12b-f**, work a treble crochet in the next single crochet and in each single crochet across. At the end of Row 14, you will have 22 treble crochets including the beginning chain 4.

ROW 15

Chain 4 (**counts as the first treble crochet**); turn your work around. Skip the first treble crochet on the previous row and work a treble crochet in the next treble crochet and in each treble crochet across to the last treble crochet (the turning chain 4 of the previous row). Work your last treble crochet in the top of the chain 4 (*Fig. 12g*). You will have 22 treble crochets.

Fig. 12g   Right-handed

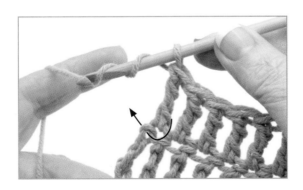

Fig. 12g   Left-handed

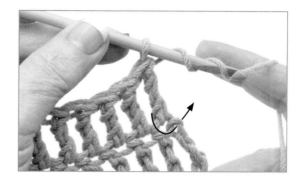

ROW 16

Repeat Row 15; at the end of the row,
you will have 22 treble crochets.

You're almost finished!

Now, to add the edging to the Spa Cloth,
you will learn how to work in a
circle called a round *(abbreviated Rnd)*.

And you will also learn a new stitch,
the slip stitch *(abbreviated slip st)*.

Turn the page to learn how to add
the edging.

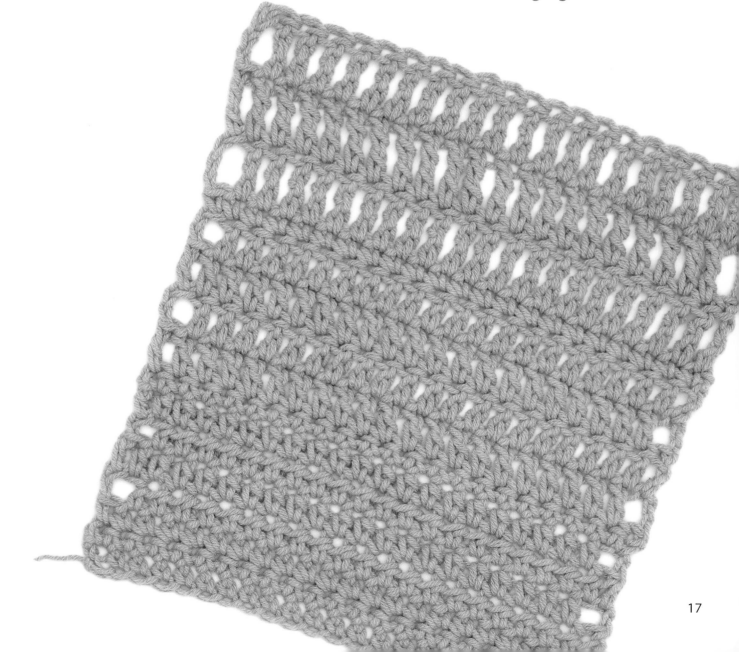

The first round of the Edging is broken down into five steps.
The Edging is easy worked step-by step!

For the Spa Cloth, working in the round means you will work single crochets across the top, down the side, across the bottom, and up the other side to the first stitch.
Just follow the instructions for Rounds 1 and 2 and you'll be done!

EDGING

ROUND 1

Chain 1; turn your work around. Work a single crochet *(Figs. 9a-c, pages 8 and 9)* in the first treble crochet and in each treble crochet across to the last treble crochet, work 3 single crochets in the last treble crochet – this forms your first corner.

Now, you will be working down the side **and** in the ends of the rows.

Work 2 single crochets in the first row, work 3 single crochets in each of the next 2 rows, skip the next single crochet row, work 2 single crochets in each of the next 4 rows, work a single crochet in the next single crochet row and in the next half double crochet row, work 2 single crochets in each of next 2 rows, work a single crochet in each of last 4 rows.

Next, you will be working across the bottom of the beginning chain. When you worked your first row of single crochets in the chain, there were loops left at the bottom edge called the "free loops." You will use these loops to work across the bottom edge of the Spa Cloth and create 2 more corners.

Remember, you can watch each technique online!
www.leisurearts.com/5947

Working in the free loops of the beginning chain *(Fig. 13)*, work 3 single crochets in the first chain (second corner made), work a single crochet in the next 20 chains, work 3 single crochets in the next chain (third corner made).

Fig. 13   Right-handed

Fig. 13   Left-handed

Now, you will be working up the opposite side of the Spa Cloth in the ends of the rows again.

Work a single crochet in the first 4 rows, work 2 single crochets in each of the next 2 rows, work a single crochet in the next half double crochet row and in the next single crochet row, work 2 single crochets in each of next 4 rows, skip the next single crochet row, work 3 single crochets in each of the next 2 rows, work 2 single crochets in the last row, work 2 single crochets in the same stitch as the first single crochet (last corner made).

You are ready to learn the slip stitch and use it to join the last stitch of your round to the first stitch.

To join the end of the round to the beginning of the round, insert your hook in the first single crochet made at the beginning of the round and bring the yarn over your hook. Pull the hook with the yarn through the stitch **and** the loop on your hook *(Fig. 14)*, completing the slip stitch.

Fig. 14   Right-handed

Fig. 14   Left-handed

To shorten instructions, a star (★) or other symbols may be used in crochet patterns. For Round 2, work the instructions after the first ★ once, then repeat the same instructions around to the joining slip stitch.

ROUND 2

Chain 1; do **not** turn your work around. ★ Work a slip stitch in the next single crochet, chain 1; repeat the instructions from the ★ around to the joining slip stitch on Round 1; work a slip stitch in the joining slip stitch.

To finish off, remove the loop from your hook. Cut the yarn leaving a 6" (15 cm) end. Bring the end through the last loop *(Fig. 15)* and tighten it.

Since both of the Edging rounds were worked with the same side of the stitches facing, that will be the "right" side of your Spa Cloth.

To hide the yarn ends on the wrong side, begin by threading a yarn needle with an end, then weave the needle in and out through the stitches *(Fig. 16)*, reversing the direction that you are weaving the end several times. Once the end is hidden, clip the yarn close to the work. Repeat with the remaining yarn end.

Fig. 15   Right-handed

Fig. 16   Right-handed

Fig. 15   Left-handed

Fig. 16   Left-handed

What an Accomplishment!

You have learned most crochet stitches and have a Spa Cloth to use as a gift!

Next, use your new skills to make a simple scarf, page 26.

On your way, take a look at pages 22-25 that explain how to read our patterns and other important information that would be helpful to your exploration of the world of crochet.

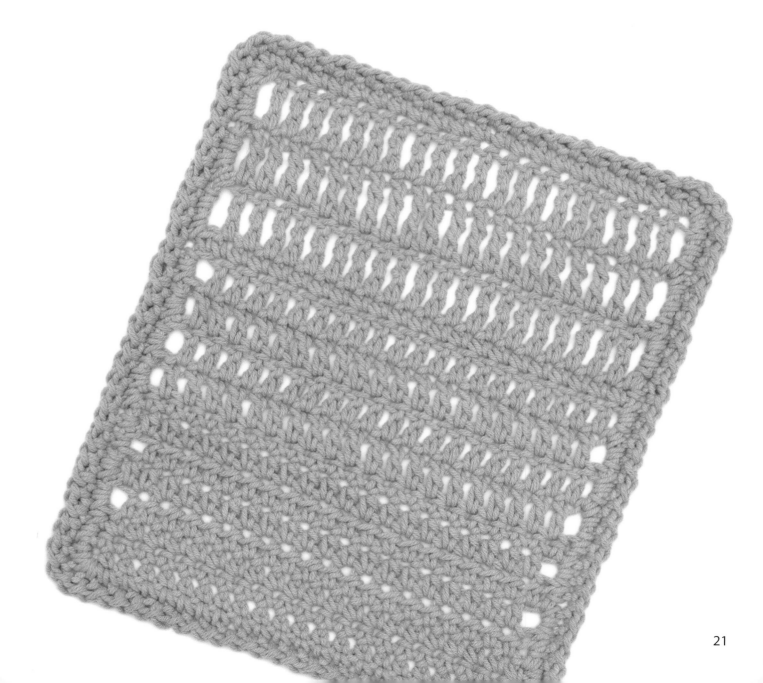

Anatomy of a pattern

Crochet instructions may look like code, full of abbreviations, punctuation marks, and other terms and symbols; but once you break them down, they are really easy. Let's take a look at a sample pattern to see all the parts.

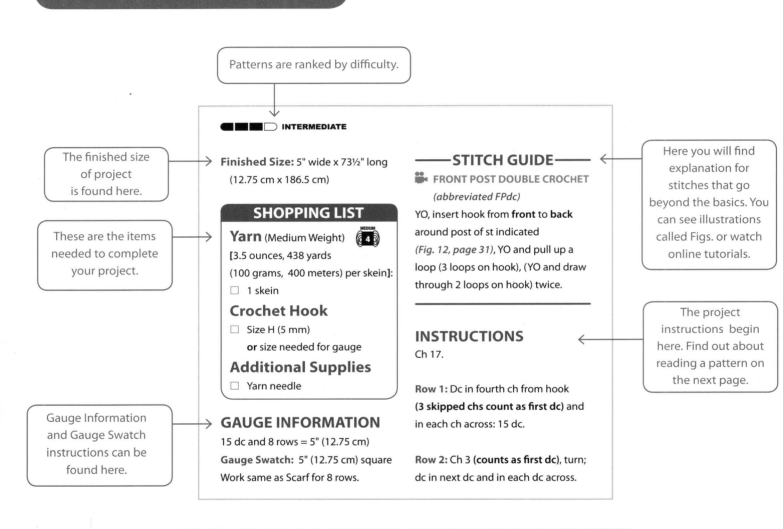

Patterns are ranked by difficulty.

■■■□ INTERMEDIATE

The finished size of project is found here.

Finished Size: 5" wide x 73½" long
(12.75 cm x 186.5 cm)

These are the items needed to complete your project.

SHOPPING LIST

Yarn (Medium Weight) (4)
[3.5 ounces, 438 yards
(100 grams, 400 meters) per skein]:
☐ 1 skein

Crochet Hook
☐ Size H (5 mm)
   or size needed for gauge

Additional Supplies
☐ Yarn needle

Gauge Information and Gauge Swatch instructions can be found here.

GAUGE INFORMATION

15 dc and 8 rows = 5" (12.75 cm)
Gauge Swatch: 5" (12.75 cm) square
Work same as Scarf for 8 rows.

───── STITCH GUIDE ─────

Here you will find explanation for stitches that go beyond the basics. You can see illustrations called Figs. or watch online tutorials.

🎥 ◄ **FRONT POST DOUBLE CROCHET**
(abbreviated FPdc)

YO, insert hook from **front** to **back** around post of st indicated *(Fig. 12, page 31)*, YO and pull up a loop (3 loops on hook), (YO and draw through 2 loops on hook) twice.

INSTRUCTIONS

Ch 17.

Row 1: Dc in fourth ch from hook **(3 skipped chs count as first dc)** and in each ch across: 15 dc.

Row 2: Ch 3 **(counts as first dc)**, turn; dc in next dc and in each dc across.

The project instructions begin here. Find out about reading a pattern on the next page.

🎥 This icon lets you know we have online videos to help with specific techniques.

How To Read A Pattern

The instructions for the Spa Cloth were written using no abbreviations at all. The sample is written in the manner of the rest of the patterns in this book.

When reading your crochet instructions in the other projects in this book, read from punctuation mark to punctuation mark. As in grammar, commas (,) and semicolons (;) mean to pause and periods (.) mean stop.

The numbers that you will find after a **colon (:)** are the number of stitches or spaces you should have at the end of the row or round you were working. This lets you know if you have worked the right number of stitches or spaces.

You will see instructions in this book that include **brackets [ ]** and **parentheses ( )**.

Parentheses ( ) can be used to indicate that several stitches are to be worked as an unit in the stitch or space indicated. For example, the V-Stitch in the Lap Robe, page 32 is defined as, "(Dc, ch 1, dc) in next st or sp." All the stitches inside the parentheses will be worked into the next stitch or space to form the V-Stitch.

Abbreviations

Here are the abbreviations used in this book:

ch(s)	chain(s)	sc	single crochet(s)
cm	centimeters	sc2tog	single crochet 2 together
dc	double crochet(s)	sp(s)	space(s)
hdc	half double crochet(s)	st(s)	stitch(es)
mm	millimeters	tr	treble crochet(s)
Rnd(s)	Round(s)	YO	yarn over

Another use of parentheses is to indicate a repetition. The instructions inside the parentheses are worked as **many** times as the number on the outside. You can find an example of this in Round 2 of the Edging of the Lap Robe, page 35: "(skip next 2 sc, work V-St in next sc) 32 times." Following these instructions, you would skip 2 single crochets and work a V-Stitch in the next single crochet, for a total of 32 times.

Brackets [ ] or parentheses may also contain explanatory remarks, such as the metric measurements after the finished sizes, or the meters of the yarn needed or a indication of the right side of a row or round.

Terms in a Pattern

Not only are there abbreviations, there are terms used that may not be familiar, such as:

right side vs. wrong side — the right side of your work is the side that will show when the piece is finished. You may be instructed to mark the right side of a piece by looping a scrap piece of yarn around a stitch on a particular row or round.

Front vs. Back — the front of a stitch is the side facing you and the back is the side away from you.

Below is a chart listing crochet terms used in the USA and abroad.

CROCHET TERMINOLOGY		
UNITED STATES		INTERNATIONAL
slip stitch (slip st)	=	single crochet (sc)
single crochet (sc)	=	double crochet (dc)
half double crochet (hdc)	=	half treble crochet (htr)
double crochet (dc)	=	treble crochet(tr)
treble crochet (tr)	=	double treble crochet (dtr)
double treble crochet (dtr)	=	triple treble crochet (ttr)
triple treble crochet (tr tr)	=	quadruple treble crochet (qtr)
skip	=	miss

What is Gauge?

Gauge is all about the size of a project. Since the size of the Spa Cloth really didn't matter, there was no gauge given for it. Notice in the Shopping List of the sample pattern on page 22 that the size of the hook is followed by the words "**or** size needed for gauge."

Gauge involves the measurement of the stitches and the rows or rounds in a specified area, such as a 4" (10 cm) square. How loosely or tightly you crochet, the size of the hook you use and the weight of the yarn will all effect the gauge. Most crochet patterns will specify a gauge that you must match for your project to turn out the intended size.

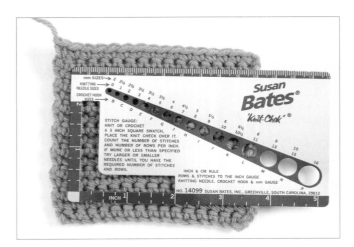

To see if you can match the gauge of a project, and ultimately the finished size, you should work the gauge swatch beforehand. If you make the swatch and it is too big, change to a smaller size hook and try again *(see Crochet Hooks chart below)*. If it turns out too small, try again with a larger size hook. Once you have found the right size hook to get the gauge, use it to crochet your project. It takes time and patience to work a gauge swatch when you want to just start crocheting, but it will save you from having an item that doesn't fit or from running out of yarn before you are finished.

Symbols in a Pattern

To shorten instructions, you will find the following symbols are commonly used.

★ — Work all the instructions following a ★ (star) as many **more** times as indicated in addition to the first time.

† to † — Work all the instructions from the first † (dagger) to the second † as **many** times as specified.

Symbols that indicate the skill levels of patterns and the yarn weights can be found on these charts.

■□□□ BEGINNER	Projects for first-time crocheters using basic stitches. Minimal shaping.
■■□□ EASY	Projects using yarn with basic stitches, repetitive stitch patterns, simple color changes, and simple shaping and finishing.
■■■□ INTERMEDIATE	Projects using a variety of techniques, such as basic lace patterns or color patterns, mid-level shaping and finishing.
■■■■ EXPERIENCED	Projects with intricate stitch patterns, techniques and dimension, such as non-repeating patterns, multi-color techniques, fine threads, small hooks, detailed shaping and refined finishing.

Yarn Weight Symbol & Names	LACE 0	SUPER FINE 1	FINE 2	LIGHT 3	MEDIUM 4	BULKY 5	SUPER BULKY 6
Type of Yarns in Category	Fingering, 10-count crochet thread	Sock, Fingering Baby	Sport, Baby	DK, Light Worsted	Worsted, Afghan, Aran	Chunky, Craft, Rug	Bulky, Roving
Crochet Gauge* Ranges in Single Crochet to 4" (10 cm)	32-42 double crochets**	21-32 sts	16-20 sts	12-17 sts	11-14 sts	8-11 sts	5-9 sts
Advised Hook Size Range	Steel*** 6,7,8 Regular hook B-1	B-1 to E-4	E-4 to 7	7 to I-9	I-9 to K-10.5	K-10.5 to M-13	M-13 and larger

*GUIDELINES ONLY: The chart above reflects the most commonly used gauges and hook sizes for specific yarn categories.

** Lace weight yarns are usually crocheted on larger-size hooks to create lacy openwork patterns. Accordingly, a gauge range is difficult to determine. Always follow the gauge stated in your pattern.

*** Steel crochet hooks are sized differently from regular hooks–the higher the number the smaller the hook, which is the reverse of regular hook sizing.

CROCHET HOOKS															
U.S.	B-1	C-2	D-3	E-4	F-5	G-6	H-8	I-9	J-10	K-10½	L-11	M/N-13	N/P-15	P/Q	Q	S
Metric - mm	2.25	2.75	3.25	3.5	3.75	4	5	5.5	6	6.5	8	9	10	15	16	19

Finishing Techniques

Weaving In Yarn Ends

Make a habit of taking care of loose ends as you work. Never tie a knot in your yarn. A knot may poke through to the right side or become untied and unravel. Weaving in the ends gives a much better result. Thread a yarn needle with the yarn end. With the **wrong** side facing, weave the needle through several stitches, then reverse the direction and weave it back through several more stitches *(Fig. 16, page 20)*. When the end is secure, clip the yarn off close to your work.

You may also hide your ends as you work by crocheting over them for several inches to secure; clip the remaining lengths off close to your work.

Always check your work to be sure the yarn ends do not show on the right side.

Working Stitches Evenly Across Or Around

When you are given a specific number of stitches to work across the ends of the rows as in the Edging of the Lap Robe, page 32, place pins or markers on one side to divide the area in three equal parts. Then, work approximately a third of the total stitches in each part. In the case of the Lap Robe, 115 stitches divided by 3 will have 38 stitches in two parts and 39 in one part to equal the 115 stitches.

When you are instructed to single crochet evenly across or around and are not given a specific number, space the single crochets in a manner to keep the piece lying flat. Work a few single crochets at a time, checking periodically to be sure that the edge is not distorted. If the edge is puckering, you need to add a few more single crochets; if the edge is ruffling, you need to remove some single crochets. Keep trying until the edge lies smooth and flat.

Blocking

Blocking helps to smooth your work and give it a professional appearance. Before blocking, check the yarn label for any special instructions because many acrylics and some blends may be damaged during blocking.

On acrylics that can be blocked, you simply pin your item to the correct size with rust-proof pins and cover the item with dampened bath towels. When the towels are dry, the item is blocked.

If the item is hand washable, carefully launder it using a mild soap or detergent. Rinse it without wringing or twisting. Remove any excess moisture by rolling it in a succession of dry towels. If you prefer, you may put it in the final spin cycle of your washer without water. Lay the item on a large towel on a flat surface out of direct sunlight. Gently smooth and pat it to the desired size and shape, comparing the measurements to the pattern instructions as necessary. When the item is completely dry, it is blocked.

Are you ready to crochet your next project?

If you need help along the way, refer back to the techniques or go online and watch our videos to see how it's done!

Simple Scarf

Use your new skills and variegated yarn to make this simple scarf! The first set of instructions uses abbreviations while the second set is written without any. Work from either one to get the same fabulous result!

⬤▢▢▢ **BEGINNER**

Finished Size: Approximately 5" x 74" (12.5 cm x 188 cm)

SHOPPING LIST

Yarn (Medium Weight)
[3 ounces, 145 yards
(85 grams, 133 meters) per skein]:
☐   2 skeins

Crochet Hook
☐   Size H (5 mm)
    or size needed for gauge

Additional Supplies
☐   Yarn needle

GAUGE INFORMATION
15 dc and 8 rows = 5" (12.75 cm)
Gauge Swatch: 5" (12.75 cm) square
Work same as Scarf for 8 rows.

INSTRUCTIONS WITH ABBREVIATIONS
Ch 17.

Row 1: Dc in fourth ch from hook **(3 skipped chs count as first dc)** and in each ch across: 15 dc.

Row 2: Ch 3 **(counts as first dc)**, turn; dc in next dc and in each dc across.

Repeat Row 2 until Scarf measures approximately 74" (188 cm) long.

Finish off.

INSTRUCTIONS WITHOUT ABBREVIATIONS
Chain 17 to start your scarf.

Row 1: Work a double crochet in the fourth chain from your hook. The three chains you just skipped will count as your first double crochet on this row. Work a double crochet in the next 13 chains. You will have 15 double crochets.

Row 2: Chain 3 **(counts as the first double crochet, now and throughout)**, turn your work around. Skip the first double crochet on the previous row and work a double crochet in the next double crochet and in each double crochet across to the last double crochet (the top of the 3 skipped chains of the first row). Work your last double crochet in the top of the chain. You will have 15 double crochets.

Row 3: Chain 3, turn your work around. Skip the first double crochet on the previous row and work a double crochet in the next double crochet and in each double crochet across to the last double crochet (the turning chain 3 of the previous row). Work your last double crochet in the top of the chain. You will have 15 double crochets.

Repeat Row 3 until you have used almost all the yarn in the first skein, stopping before working the last 2 loops of the last double crochet. Leave the loops on your hook *(Fig. 17a)*.

Fig. 17a Right-handed

Fig. 17a Left-handed

Cut the old yarn, leaving a 6" (15 cm) end. Leaving a 6" (15 cm) end of the new yarn, bring yarn over your hook and draw through both loops on the hook, completing the last double crochet *(Fig. 17b)*.

Fig. 17b   Right-handed

Fig. 17b   Left-handed

Continue repeating Row 3 until the Scarf measures approximately 74" (188 cm). At the end of the last row, cut your yarn and finish off.

Weave in the yarn ends.

You can go back to pages 12 through 14 to review the double crochet stitch or watch the tutorial online!

Scarf

This keyhole scarf is the perfect way to learn how to shape by increasing and decreasing. If you need help with the abbreviations, look for them on page 23.

 **EASY +**

Finished Size:

6½" x 33" (16.5 cm x 84 cm)

SHOPPING LIST

Yarn (Medium Weight)

[2.5 ounces, 175 yards (70 grams, 160 meters) per skein]:

☐ Variegated - 1 skein

Crochet Hook

☐ Size K (6.5 mm)

or size needed for gauge

Additional Supplies

☐ Safety pin

GAUGE INFORMATION

(Sc, ch 1) 4 times = 2" (5 cm)

5 rows = 1½" (3.75 cm)

Gauge Swatch: 6½"w x 4"h (16.5 cm x 10 cm)

Work same as Scarf through Row 12: 14 sc and 11 ch-1 sps.

STITCH GUIDE

BEGINNING SINGLE CROCHET 2 TOGETHER

(abbreviated beginning sc2tog) (uses first sc and next ch-1 sp)

Pull up a loop in first sc **and** in next ch-1 sp *(Fig. 18a)*, YO and draw through all 3 loops on hook *(Fig. 18b)* **(counts as one sc).**

Fig. 18a Right-handed

Fig. 18a Left-handed

Fig. 18b Right-handed

Fig. 18b Left-handed

ENDING SINGLE CROCHET 2 TOGETHER

(abbreviated ending sc2tog) (uses last ch-1 sp and last sc)

Pull up a loop in last ch-1 sp **and** in last sc *(Fig. 19a)*, YO and draw through all 3 loops on hook *(Fig. 19b)* **(counts as one sc).**

Fig. 19a Right-handed

Fig. 19a Left-handed

Fig. 19b Right-handed

Fig. 19b Left-handed

🎥 JOINING WITH SINGLE CROCHET

Begin with slip knot on your hook *(Fig. 20a)*. Insert hook in sc indicated, YO and pull up a loop, YO and draw though both loops on hook *(Fig. 20b)*.

Fig. 20a Right-handed   Fig. 20a Left-handed

Fig. 20b Right-handed   Fig. 20b Left-handed

Remember, you can watch each technique online!
www.leisurearts.com/5947

INSTRUCTIONS

Note: To make the opening in the Scarf, Rows 23-28 are worked in two separate parts. Before beginning the Scarf, wind 5 yards (4.5 meters) into a ball to use for the Second Part of Rows 23-28.

Row 1 (Right side)**:** Ch 2, 3 sc in second ch from hook: 3 sc.

Note: Loop a short piece of yarn around any stitch to mark Row 1 as **right** side.

Row 2: Ch 1, turn; 2 sc in first sc, ch 1, skip next sc, 2 sc in last sc: 4 sc and one ch-1 sp.

Row 3: Ch 1, turn; 2 sc in first sc, ch 1, skip next sc, sc in next ch-1 sp, ch 1, skip next sc, 2 sc in last sc: 5 sc and 2 ch-1 sps.

Rows 4-13 (Increase rows)**:** Ch 1, turn; 2 sc in first sc, ch 1, (skip next sc, sc in next ch-1 sp, ch 1) across to last 2 sc, skip next sc, 2 sc in last sc: 15 sc and 12 ch-1 sps.

Row 14: Ch 1, turn; sc in first sc, ch 1, (skip next sc, sc in next ch-1 sp, ch 1) across to last 2 sc, skip next sc, sc in last sc: 14 sc and 13 ch-1 sps.

Rows 15-22 (Decrease rows)**:** Ch 1, turn; work beginning sc2tog, ch 1, skip next sc, (sc in next ch-1 sp, ch 1, skip next sc) across to last ch-1 sp, work ending sc2tog: 6 sc and 5 ch-1 sps.

Row 23 - First Part: Ch 1, turn; sc in first sc and in next ch-1 sp, ch 1, skip next sc, sc in next ch-1 sp and in next sc, leave remaining 3 sc and 3 ch-1 sps unworked: 4 sc and 1 ch-1 sp.

Row 24 - First Part: Ch 1, turn; sc in first sc, ch 1, skip next sc, sc in next ch-1 sp, ch 1, skip next sc, sc in last sc: 3 sc and 2 ch-1 sps.

Row 25 - First Part: Ch 1, turn; sc in first sc and in next ch-1 sp, ch 1, skip next sc, sc in next ch-1 sp and in last sc: 4 sc and one ch-1 sp.

Rows 26 thru 28 - First Part: Repeat Rows 24 and 25 once, then repeat Row 24 once **more**.

Do **not** finish off. Slip loop from hook onto safety pin to keep the piece from unraveling so that you may work Second Part.

Row 23 - Second Part: With **right** side facing, skip first unworked ch-1 sp on Row 22 and join yarn from small ball with sc in next unworked sc; sc in next ch-1 sp, ch 1, skip next sc, sc in next ch-1 sp and in last sc: 4 sc and one ch-1 sp.

Row 24 - Second Part: Ch 1, turn; sc in first sc, ch 1, skip next sc, sc in next ch-1 sp, ch 1, skip next sc, sc in last sc: 3 sc and 2 ch-1 sps.

Row 25 - Second Part: Ch 1, turn; sc in first sc and in next ch-1 sp, ch 1, skip next sc, sc in next ch-1 sp and in last sc: 4 sc and one ch-1 sp.

Rows 26 thru 28 - Second Part: Repeat Rows 24 and 25 once, then repeat Row 24 once **more**.

Finish off.

Row 29 (Joining row)**:** With **right** side facing, slip loop from safety pin onto hook, ch 1, sc in first sc and in next ch-1 sp, ch 1, skip next sc, sc in next ch-1 sp and in next sc, ch 1, sc in first sc on Second Part and in next ch-1 sp, ch 1, skip next sc, sc in next ch-1 sp and in last sc: 8 sc and 3 ch-1 sps.

Row 30 (Increase row)**:** Ch 1, turn; 2 sc in first sc, ch 1, skip next sc, sc in next ch-1 sp, ch 1, skip next sc, sc in next sc, ch 1, skip next ch-1 sp, sc in next sc, ch 1, skip next sc, sc in next ch-1 sp, ch 1, skip next sc, 2 sc in last sc: 8 sc and 5 ch-1 sps.

Rows 31-37 (Increase rows)**:** Ch 1, turn; 2 sc in first sc, ch 1, (skip next sc, sc in next ch-1 sp, ch 1) across to last 2 sc, skip next sc, 2 sc in last sc: 15 sc and 12 ch-1 sps.

Row 38: Ch 1, turn; sc in first sc, ch 1, (skip next sc, sc in next ch-1 sp, ch 1) across to last 2 sc, skip next sc, sc in last sc: 14 sc and 13 ch-1 sps.

Row 39: Ch 1, turn; sc in first sc and in next ch-1 sp, (ch 1, skip next sc, sc in next ch-1 sp) across to last sc, sc in last sc: 15 sc and 12 ch-1 sps.

Rows 40-72: Repeat Rows 38 and 39, 16 times; then repeat Row 38 once **more**: 14 sc and 13 ch-1 sps.

Rows 73-80 (Decrease rows)**:** Ch 1, turn; work beginning sc2tog, ch 1, skip next sc, (sc in next ch-1 sp, ch 1, skip next sc) across to last ch-1 sp, work ending sc2tog: 6 sc and 5 ch-1 sps.

Row 81: Ch 1, turn; sc in first sc and in next ch-1 sp, (ch 1, skip next sc, sc in next ch-1 sp) 4 times, sc in last sc: 7 sc and 4 ch-1 sps.

Row 82: Ch 1, turn; sc in first sc, ch 1, (skip next sc, sc in next ch-1 sp, ch 1) 4 times, skip next sc, sc in last sc: 6 sc and 5 ch-1 sps.

Rows 83-87: Repeat Rows 81 and 82 twice, then repeat Row 81 once **more**: 7 sc and 4 ch-1 sps.

Rows 88-95 (Increase rows)**:** Ch 1, turn; 2 sc in first sc, ch 1, (skip next sc, sc in next ch-1 sp, ch 1) across to last 2 sc, skip next sc, 2 sc in last sc: 15 sc and 12 ch-1 sps.

Row 96: Ch 1, turn; sc in first sc, ch 1, (skip next sc, sc in next ch-1 sp, ch 1) across to last 2 sc, skip next sc, sc in last sc: 14 sc and 13 ch-1 sps.

Rows 97-106 (Decrease rows)**:** Ch 1, turn; work beginning sc2tog, ch 1, skip next sc, (sc in next ch-1 sp, ch 1, skip next sc) across to last ch-1 sp, work ending sc2tog: 4 sc and 3 ch-1 sps.

Row 107: Ch 1, turn; work beginning sc2tog, ch 1, skip next sc, sc in next ch-1 sp, ch 1, skip next sc, work ending sc2tog: 3 sc and 2 ch-1 sps.

Row 108: Ch 1, turn; work beginning sc2tog, ch 1, skip next sc, work ending sc2tog: 2 sc and one ch-1 sp.

Row 109: Ch 1, turn; pull up a loop in first sc **and** in next ch-1 sp **and** in last sc, YO and draw through all 4 loops on hook; finish off.

Design by Carol L. Jensen.

By working with a solid color yarn, you can achieve an entirely different look to this scarf pattern!

Lacy Lap Robe

Learn two different ways to change to another color of yarn with this easy, lacy lap robe!

 **EASY**

Finished Size: 29" x 38"

(73.5 cm x 96.5 cm)

SHOPPING LIST

Yarn (Medium Weight)

[3.5 ounces, 208 yards

(100 grams, 190 meters) per skein]:

- ☐ Blue - 3 skeins
- ☐ Cream - 2 skeins

Crochet Hook

- ☐ Size I (5.5 mm)

  or size needed for gauge

GAUGE INFORMATION

In pattern,

5 V-Sts and 8 rows = 4" (10 cm)

Gauge Swatch: 4" (10 cm) square

With Blue, ch 17.

Rows 1-8: Work same as Body,

page 34: 15 dc.

Finish off.

STITCH GUIDE

🎥 **V-STITCH** (abbreviated V-St)

(Dc, ch 1, dc) in st or sp indicated.

Right-handed

Left-handed

🎥 **JOINING WITH SINGLE CROCHET**

Begin with slip knot on your hook (*Fig. 21a*). Insert hook in dc indicated, YO and pull up a loop, YO and draw though both loops on hook (*Fig. 21b*).

Fig. 21a Right-handed

Fig. 21a Left-handed

Fig. 21b Right-handed

Fig. 21b Left-handed

CHANGING COLORS

Work last dc to within one step of completion (last 2 loops on hook) *(Fig. 22a)*. Drop old color, with new color, YO and draw though both loops on hook *(Fig. 22b)*.

Fig. 22a Right-handed

Fig. 22a Left-handed

Fig. 22b Right-handed

Fig. 22b Left-handed

INSTRUCTIONS
BODY

With Blue, ch 101.

Row 1: Dc in fifth ch from hook **(beginning V-St made)**, (skip next 2 chs, work V-St in next ch) across: 33 V-Sts.

Row 2 (Right side)**:** Ch 3 **(counts as first dc, now and throughout)**, turn; 2 dc in first V-St (ch-1 sp), 3 dc in next V-St and in each V-St across, changing to Cream in last dc made; cut Blue: 99 dc.

Note: Loop a short piece of yarn around any stitch to mark Row 2 as **right** side.

Row 3: Ch 1, turn; sc in first dc, ch 3, sc in next dc, (ch 3, skip next 2 dc, sc in next dc) across to last dc, leave last dc unworked: 33 ch-3 sps.

Row 4: Ch 5, turn; skip first sc, sc in next ch-3 sp, (ch 3, skip next sc, sc in next ch-3 sp) across to last sc, leave last sc unworked.

Rows 5 and 6: Ch 5, turn; skip first sc, sc in next ch-3 sp, (ch 3, skip next sc, sc in next ch-3 sp) across to last sc, ch 3, skip last sc, sc in last ch-5 sp.

Finish off.

Row 7: With **wrong** side facing, join Blue with slip st in first ch-3 sp, ch 4, dc in same sp **(counts as first V-St, now and throughout)**, work V-st in next ch-3 sp and in each ch-sp across: 33 V-Sts.

Row 8: Ch 3, turn; 2 dc in first V-St, 3 dc in next V-St and in each V-St across, changing to Cream in last dc made; cut Blue: 99 dc.

Row 9: Ch 1, turn; sc in first dc, ch 3, sc in next dc, (ch 3, skip next 2 dc, sc in next dc) across to last dc, leave last dc unworked: 33 ch-3 sps.

Row 10: Ch 5, turn; skip first sc, sc in next ch-3 sp, (ch 3, skip next sc, sc in next ch-3 sp) across to last sc, leave last sc unworked; finish off.

Row 11: With **wrong** side facing, join Blue with slip st in first ch-3 sp; ch 4, dc in same sp, work V-st in next ch-3 sp and in each ch-sp across: 33 V-Sts.

Row 12: Ch 3, turn; 2 dc in first V-St, 3 dc in next V-St and in each V-St across, changing to Cream in last dc made; cut Blue: 99 dc.

Rows 13-82: Repeat Rows 3-12, 7 times; at end of Row 82, do **not** change to Cream and do **not** cut Blue.

EDGING

Rnd 1: Ch 1, do **not** turn; 🎥 work 115 sc evenly spaced across ends of rows to last row, 3 sc in last row; 🎥 working in free loops of beginning ch *(Fig. 13, page 19)*, sc in ch at base of first V-St and in each ch across; 3 sc in end of first row, work 115 sc evenly spaced across ends of rows; working in sts across Row 82, sc in first dc, place a marker in sc just made for st placement, 2 sc in same dc, sc in next dc and in each dc across to last dc, 3 sc in last dc; join with slip st to first sc, finish off: 436 sc.

Rnd 2: With **right** side facing, join Tan with slip st in marked sc; ch 4, dc in same st, work V-St in next sc, † (skip next 2 sc, work V-St in next sc) 32 times, skip next 2 sc, work V-St in each of next 2 sc, (skip next 2 sc, work V-St in next sc) 38 times, skip next 2 sc †, work V-St in each of next 2 sc, repeat from † to † once; join with slip st to third ch of beginning ch-4: 148 V-Sts.

Rnd 3: Slip st in first V-St, ch 3, 2 dc in same sp, 3 dc in next V-St and in each V-St around; join with slip st to first dc, finish off.

Rnd 4: With **right** side facing, join Blue with sc in any dc; sc in next dc and in each dc around, working 3 sc in each corner dc; join with slip st to first sc, finish off.

Design by Joyce Winfield Vanderslice.

Yarn Information

Projects in this book were made with medium weight yarn. Any brand of medium weight of yarn may be used. It is best to refer to yardage/meters when determining how many balls or skeins to purchase. Remember, to arrive at the finished size, it is the GAUGE/TENSION that is important, not the brand of yarn. For your convenience, listed below are the specific colors used to create our photography models.

SPA CLOTH
Lion Brand® Cotton-Ease®
#123 Seaspray

SCARF
Red Heart® Boutique™ Eclipse™
#9851 Tidal Wave

SIMPLE SCARF
Lion Brand® Vanna's Choice®
#203 Autumn Print

LACY LAP ROBE
Patons® Decor
Blue - #87206 New Teal
Cream - #87630 Pale Taupe

Remember, you can watch each technique online!
www.leisurearts.com/5947

Your opinion matters!

WE WOULD LOVE TO HEAR if our online video instructions and the new format of our publications are helpful to you!

PLEASE SHARE your comments and suggestions at
www.facebook.com/Official.LeisureArts

At Leisure Arts, we're excited about bringing you the most complete, easy-to-follow instructions. Let us know how we can make your creative experiences more fun, more rewarding--and yes, even easier!

We have made every effort to ensure that these instructions are accurate and complete. We cannot, however, be responsible for human error, typographical mistakes, or variations in individual work.

PRODUCTION TEAM: Writer/Technical Editor - Sarah J. Green; Editorial Writer - Susan Frantz Wiles; Graphic Artists - Stacy Owens and Becca Snider Tally; Senior Graphic Artist - Lora Puls; Photo Stylists - Brooke Duszota and Christy Myers; and Photographers - Jason Masters and Ken West.

Items made and instructions tested by Marianna Crowder.